# SECRETS BEHIND THE FOUR WALLS
and the Monster Mom that Lived Inside Them

# SECRETS
### Behind the
# FOUR WALLS
and the Monster Mom That Lived Inside Them

by Rani

INKWATER PRESS

PORTLAND • OREGON
INKWATERPRESS.COM

Scan this QR Code
to learn more about
this title

Copyright © 2014 by Rani

Cover and interior design by Jayme Vincent

© Aprescindere. DreamsTime.com

All rights reserved. No part of this book may be reproduced or transmitted in any form or by any means whatsoever, including photocopying, recording or by any information storage and retrieval system, without written permission from the publisher and/or author. Contact Inkwater Press at 6750 SW Franklin Street, Suite A, Portland, OR 97223-2542. 503.968.6777

Publisher: Inkwater Press | www.inkwaterpress.com

Paperback
ISBN-13 978-1-62901-005-2 | ISBN-10 1-62901-005-7

Kindle
ISBN-13 978-1-62901-006-9 | ISBN-10 1-62901-006-5

Printed in the U.S.A.
All paper is acid free and meets all ANSI standards for archival quality paper.

3 5 7 9 10 8 6 4 2

My dedication goes to God,
Jesus, the Messiah, the King of Kings.
I want to thank my Daughter Tiffany
and my Son Giovanni for seeing me through
my trials and tribulation.

I was born November 8th 1965. I grew up in a 2 parent home with my older brother David. My Dad worked for the West Seattle News Paper, Mom was a fashion illustrator for Nordstrom. They loved to dance and entertain friends on the weekends. Dad would take myself, my brother and all the neighborhood kids to the local park on Saturdays. We would climb trees and explore the woods. We all had a great time. Dad loved steaks in front of the t.v. watching "Nightmare Theater" on Saturday nights and delicious, pancakes and eggs Sunday morning. Mom and Dad would sometimes sit at the dining room table and work on her fashion illustrations that were deadlined for the next morning. Mom valued Dads

# Rani

opinion because he was such a smart and talented man as well as a great father.

My whole world fell apart around 1972 when Dad met a younger woman and started an affair behind moms back. When Mom found out she was devastated and kicked him out of the house and almost out of our lives. Dad moved into a studio apartment in West Seattle. On one rainy afternoon Mom drag me over to Dads apartment and we heard him and his new girlfriend having a good ol' time. Mom started pounding on the door and all hell broke loose. This was not the first nor the last time she would drag me into their mess. We found Dad and his girlfriend again at a Chinese Restaurant and once again Mom started screaming and yelling at them causing a scene. I remember her pooring hot tea all over Dads girlfriends lap. Needless to say...we were escorted out of the restaurant.

Mom drove home very fast and very angry. She drove her 1965 Thunderbird straight into our backyard fence, knocking it down and embarrassing the hell out of my 7 year old soul. She stormed inside our house, leaving me in the running car with all eyes on me from our curious neighbors. They all came out of their homes to see what the loud noise was. It was so scary. Mostly embarrassing because all of my neighborhood friends finally knew my home was very different than theirs. From that time on Mom wouldn't let me see Dad nor let him see my Brother either.

I remember one very late night, while sleeping, my dad snuck into the house to see my Brother and I. We were so happy to see each other. Dad brought us a small black and white t.v for our bedroom which would later on be my only source of company.

Around this time my Mom started drinking heavily and getting verbally and physically abusive with my then 9 year old Brother. I can't quite remember if I was also getting abused at this time.

Moms drinking and abuse got so bad that my Brothers teacher and principle of our school came to our home to confront her. If my Brother complained that his shoes hurt or they had holes in them, Mom would cut a stick from the backyard and beat my Brothers feet and toes until they bled. On the nights she was drinking heavily she would yell and beat my Brother for hours. He would have to get up the next morning and go to school in that horrific condition. The teacher started noticing him coming to school with blood in his hair, bruises all over and a limp in his step. After a while it became obvious to the school that something was horribly wrong in our home.

In the 1970s Parents ruled with an Iron Fist but the school knew this was not a normal "I'm just

## Rani

disciplining my child" situation. David was taken out of our home and moved to Centrailia WA to live with our Grandparents for around 6 months. While gone he joined a Youth Group and was involved in Church and also was doing great in school. When David returned home, Mom convinced us things would get better but in no time at all her drinking and abuse returned with a vengeance.

Mom was cruel, Evil and even "Demon like" most of the time. Mom started blaming David for Dad leaving and them getting a divorce. Mom would yell "It's your fault your Dad left his family". To me it seemed this never ended. The abuse took a bizarre turn when Mom would lock David up in an old shed that was in the lower 40 of our backyard. It was a wood shed that Dad use to keep yard tools and paint in. It had 2 small windows and one door. David never had to do much to get locked up in the shed. If she thought he gave a dirty look or as she would say he "flipped" or "flippen off" it was in the shed he went. Mom would lock him in for hours which turned into days and sometimes a week. He would at times be wearing clothes or sometimes be completely naked. Being naked at 10 to 11 years old for a young boy was very humiliating which was just what Mom was going for.

After a night of torcher, she would finally pass out

# Secrets Behind the Four Walls
## and the Monster Mother That Lived Inside Them

giving us the sense of peace and relief. After I knew it was safe and I wouldn't get caught, I would make the long trip down the lower 40 to the shed only lit my moonlight. If there was no moon to light the way it was pitch dark. I would talk to my Brother through the locked door. He would never allow me to let him out saying "if we get caught, it will only get worse".

David got locked in the shed on his birthday after a night of being told he was worthless, she wishes he was never born and beaten black and blue. He was again sent to the shed naked, bruised and ashamed. After mom passed out, I wanted to do something for him on his birthday. I wrapped some of Davids own clothes up as a present, a white tee shirt, one pair of brown corduroy pants and a pair of socks with holes in the toes and a pair of shoes a size too small. After I wrapped them all and put a pretty bow I made a card with crayons. On the front of the card there was a birthday cake with candles. On the inside I drew us holding hands. I was too young to write at this point so pictures explained what I was trying to say. I took the long, dark, scary trip to the shed after feeling it was safe with my gifts in hand. I said "David I have some presents for you for your birthday." He opened the door partially covering his naked body that he did not want me seeing. I handed him the presents.

## Rani

He closed the door and I locked it. I heard him say "Thanks". He dressed himself in the clothes, came out and gave me a hug, and then told me to and get back in the house so Mom does not find out. "This was our secret and don't tell Mom anything."

I ran up to the back of the house, tip toed to my room and went to bed, while David slept in the cold oh so scary, oh so dark and damp shed on this cold, damp night, his Birthday, all alone. I still remember to this day, how horrible I felt leaving my Brother in that cold, dark and scary shed. I was also relieved that I somehow did something nice for my brother David on his Birthday which was April 3rd.

Mom was not working at this time so she would be there when we got home from school. She would always be on her way to drunk and mad about something. It would be as little as two socks in our dresser that did not match. We never knew who she would be when we got home. David would arrive home a half hour after I did. David rode the school bus. Mom and I would watch David get off the bus and walk with the other kids to the house. She would yell to me "Just wait tell he gets home". I was always so scared for David and I'm sure he was scared to come home, never knowing what was in store for him.

Most of the time he was met with yelling and

screaming about nothing and a tall glass of liquid Ivory soap to try and gulp down with just a little glass of water. A long stick was also waiting that had previously been cut from a Lilac tree in the backyard. Mom would hand David the glass of liquid soap and told me to watch and make sure he drank it all. This became a ritual. Most of the time he would drink it crying in agony. He was made to do this so much that his mouth and throat became raw. After a while it was almost impossible so I would poor out the liquid soap behind the stereo consul we had in our living room. Afterword David would stand in the corner for hours until Mom told him to go to his room.

After time went on you couldn't even vacuum behind the stereo because all the soap build up. Mom never knew I did this. David had a hard time eating or drinking due to the ritual of drinking the liquid soap all the time for doing nothing. He never did anything at all to deserve the abuse he endured. He did absolutely NOTHING!

Mom would think of more and more ways to humiliate and abuse my brother. She had an art board with a large art light attached to it. She would move the art board into the middle of the living room. She would turn all the lights off in the house except the large art light attached to the art board. Mom would

# RANI

make David stand under the large, spot light completely naked. He was made to stand there while she called him a liar and stupid. He would constantly get blamed for why Dad left. She would ask him the same questions over and over again, knowing he didn't have the answers. She would repeatedly hit him upside his head and slap him in the face. It got so bad one winter night he ran outside stark naked into the snow at 1am in a cold, dark morning to hide in the backyard. Mom was yelling for him but he stayed out there for as long as he could cold, wet and scared. After bring him a blanket, I tried calming mom down and was successful that night due to the tranquilizer pills she took.

This is the house I grew up in
As you can see, it is all closed up. It was always
all closed up to hide what was going on inside
(childhood friend)

## Secrets Behind the Four Walls
### and the Monster Mother That Lived Inside Them

Off to school the next day, David would always have to ask me "can you see this" meaning blood, cuts or bruises from the hours of abuse the night before.

Mom upped the abuse to an all-time high Christmas Day mom flew into a rage over something she made up in her own head. She flung his bedroom door open and David was sitting on his bed reading a comic book. Mom took the heavy Hoover Vacuum cleaner and swung it at Davids head, splitting it wide open. Mom also broke the mirror at the end of the hallway telling David to clean it up as he was bleeding from his head. Afterwards he was to get back into his room for the rest of Christmas. Mom threw all his Christmas gifts in his room and told him there would be no Christmas dinner for him. "Don't come out of this room, not even to go to the bathroom" she screamed. For almost a day in a half he was not allowed any food or bathroom privileges. He wet himself which he didn't want Mom knowing. Of course she did and came up with the ultimate punishment for this

Mom made David walk around in a diaper she made from a sheet only pinned with safety pins and told him he would have to wear this to school. Thank God we were on Christmas vacation. By this time Dad was living with his new girlfriend. David told Dad what had been going on at home and he was taken to the doctor. He had several severe injuries and suffered 8 concussions that went untreated.

Knowing this and the Doctors reports, Dad wanted us out of the house of Torment. He got us out as quickly as he could. Dad took us into hiding. We were shuffled around to a few different homes. David and I were separated at this time. My hair and name were changed and even my school. Dad had positioned the court for custody. Brother and I had to give a statement in court. David did and I did not. I was very young and very scared. I couldn't go against my mom. Dad was not happy with me. Dad got David and mom got me.

Mom came, took me into the car and I went home with her. David went to stay with our Grandparents in Centralia once again. Life was great for David finally and I missed him. Now it was a house of horrors for Rani.

Mom had met a younger man 19 years her junior. She met him down at a bar on Alki Beach around 1978. They fell for each other instantly. He had 3 daughters around my age. She seemed happy at this time. The girls would stay over on the weekends when Ron had visitation. Ron would pick the girls up and drop them off with Mom. It was more like our visitation then Ron's. Mom very soon started showing favoritism towards them using that to hurt me. One weekend she let them sleep in my room after having a nice dinner, excluding me. I had to sleep outside with one blanket and in the rain. I'm not sure what I did to deserve this. Even the dog got fed and was able to sleep inside. One night while sleeping outside under the picture frame window in front of the house Mom flung open the front door and told me to get in the house. It was around 3 in the morning and she needed me to help her put foil on her bedroom window. There was always foil on her bedroom window. I was trying to help her but she kept yelling at me to stay quiet so I wouldn't wake the girls sleeping peacefully in my bed and in my bedroom.

She kept slapping me in the face and hitting me in the head. Looking back, I suspect she was using more than just alcohol at the time, maybe there was always more than just alcohol. I had no idea I just knew this was different. The next morning the girls got out of bed and opened the front door to let me in, all the while making fun of the fact I had to sleep outside. "Oh your mom loves us more", "your room is now our room", "and your stuff is now our stuff", "go back outside dog". This hurt and humiliated me. Mom would always do for the girls and not for me and I never knew why. I just thought it was her way of making Ron like her more.

Ron would show up every now and again, after

# Rani

being out all night at the bars he would knock on Moms bedroom window and she would let him in our house. I hated when he would come over. When they were finished doing what they were doing which was OBVIOUS, I would always have to plug my ears and hum. Ron would make his way into my room, sit on my bed completely naked from head to toe and try and pull the blankets off me.

He was always peaking in the hole he made in the wall that separated my room from my Moms room. He would constantly watch me through that hole, I hated it. Mom never did anything about Ron's despicable behavior so I started sleeping on the couch. Ron would come looking for me all naked and aroused and ask me "how do I look" When I told him I was going to tell mom he would just laugh and walk away. This went on for 11 years of my life.

Mom was now beating me, verbally abusing me, and treating me like the house maid. She never got up to get her own fork, beer or drink. She never made her own bed or even did any of the yard work. One summer afternoon while the neighborhood kids were out running through sprinklers and playing, I was mowing the lawn, weeding, clipping and pruning. On one occasion I was left outside all night because I did not finish in time so Mom turned all the lights off, locked the

## Secrets Behind the Four Walls
### and the Monster Mother That Lived Inside Them

doors and went to bed. I slept outside with nothing to eat or drink. Thank God for the water hose and facet because it was summer.

On one of the nights I had to sleep outside, usually under the front window because I felt safe there, a neighbor saw me sleeping there. She was getting home late from a night out and she came and asked if I was alright and locked out. I am not sure what excuse I gave but it couldn't of sounded reasonable coming from a 8-9 year old. The neighbor Kathy said "I'm going to call your mom". I knew for a fact that would make things worse for me. Mom would blame me and think I ran and told the neighbors our "private secret." Yes the neighbor called, and yes mom got mad. It got a WHOLE LOT WORSE.

Now it was my turn to get locked up in the shed. It was not as bad as it had been with David but after a night of Mom drinking, blasting Janis Joplin on the stereo, she decided to pull me out of my room and said "I want to talk to you". I knew it was going to be a long night. I never knew when I went to sleep if I would be woken to a drunken, all night rage filled rant. How my Dads girlfriend was a whore, a home wrecker and how she took Dad away from us. It would turn into Mom wanting to go to Dads house and throw battery acid into Dads girlfriends face. How she deserved it and

# Rani

how funny that would be. This would go on and on for hours and hours all throughout the night.

If I dosed off while sitting there she would slap me in the face or hit me in the head and get more enraged. What made it even more traumatic is this would happen while all the lights were off in the house only eerily lit by the street light that came through the cracks in the curtain. Mom would always ask me "do you think Marilyn is a whore, "don't you think she deserves it". I never knew how to answer those questions. On one of moms' vengeful nights I made the mistake of saying I liked Lynn and loved Dad which needless to say turned out to be a huge mistake.

Oh my Lord did she turn into the Devil and I swore her head spun around a few times. Her eyes turned black and I just sat there frozen in Dads old orange chair that he would sit in and watch football. She jumped up and hit me over and over again with this heavy ashtray. I tried blocking my head which made her mad so she hit harder and harder. That was my first night in the shed with only my panties and slippers on.

Mom locked me in and stomped back up to the house. I crawled up on the cold, wood, work bench and watched to make sure she didn't come back. I knew if she did it would start all over again. I spent

# Secrets Behind the Four Walls
## and the Monster Mother That Lived Inside Them

2 days in that shed, no food, no water, no clothes, no company. It was lonely yet peaceful. There was a cat that lived under the shed and she would cry at night which frightened me. I thought she was hurting or dying. As an adult I realize she must have been in heat.

After 2 days, mom came down to get me, Ron was coming over with the girls and she needed me to go grocery shopping and clean the house. Mom put on a nice day for Ron and the girls full of fried chicken, potato salad and cool aid frozen pops for dessert.

I started going to Bible Study once a week if mom let me go. It was held at the neighbor's house. That same neighbor would also take us all to Sunday school. I started learning more about Jesus and the Bible and I loved it. I enjoyed it so much because I felt so safe and happy inside. This was great for me because no matter if I was in the shed, hit with a stick, or locked outside I was never alone. I would talk to God and that made everything else disappear.

When Dad called, Mom would always be the first to talk to him. They would arrange our visitation which was usually on the weekends. I looked forward to going to his apartment in West Seattle. I loved talking to Dad and hearing the plans he had made for us. The weekend couldn't come fast enough. One Saturday Dad showed up and Mom was in one of her moods

# Rani

and had the whole house closed up on a beautiful, sunny, Saturday afternoon and Dad started knocking on the door. My little orange suitcase and I were more than ready to go. I had looked forward all week even though Mom threatened all week she was going to call Dad and tell him I couldn't go that weekend.

I could hear the knocks getting louder and Dad yelling "Shelly, open the door! I'm here to pick Rani up". My mom was sitting on the couch, 2 feet from the door telling me "you don't really want to go with Rick, do you?" I would say "Yes" in a quivering, low voice and she ask again…wanting me to say no. I still said "Yes". That's when she slapped me in the face and I cried. She got mad and told me to stop crying. All the while Dad was pounding on the front door. I'm sure he thought something was wrong. Mom told me not to take one step towards the door in a deep voice. Mom pulled herself together, and threw my suitcase at me and said "have a good time". I was free! I knew what went on inside the 4 walls stayed in those 4 walls otherwise I would pay the price. I never told.

Mom would always tell me what goes on in these four walls stays in these four walls. I was not allowed to discuss this with anyone. After a beating this would be reinforced. Not sure if she ever said this to David. I do know that Mom hated when David said "I'm

# SECRETS BEHIND THE FOUR WALLS
## and the Monster Mother That Lived Inside Them

sorry". She never wanted to hear that. She said "Don't say Sorry, because it will just happen again". We never really knew what exactly "IT" was. There was no rational where she was concerned. After returning home from Dads, Mom had dinner on and the house cleaned and she wasn't too drunk… all this just to throw Dad off. After Dad left I followed mom into the kitchen. I had a fear in my stomach which I always had around my mom, never when I was around my Dad. I was afraid to have a good time over at my dad's because Mom was always in my head. Well here it comes the make it or break it question. Mom asked, "Did you have a good time?" I knew what I should have said though too young to know better, I said "Yes" in a slow, quivering voice. OH NO. The next question "do you like Marilyn" dads girlfriend. I was pouring milk into a glass at the same time I said in a low quivering voice "yes". I just knew that was going to make her mad.

You would of thought the world came to an end. Mom hit the gallon of milk out of my hands and I fell from the chair I was standing on. Mom was screaming things I could not understand as I stood in fear, I was frozen in place. She had a large, steak fork in her hand and she threw it. It bounced from the floor into my leg and stuck there. She paused for a moment, and then

# Rani

pulled the fork from my leg. I was bleeding pretty bad from the 3 large holes in my little leg. I didn't cry I just kept saying in a low calm voice "it's ok mom". Mom took me into the bathroom to put iodine and 2 large band aids on the very large holes I now had in my legs. She told me to go to get in my room and go to bed. I was ok with that even though it was a beautiful, summer evening and I could hear all my friends outside playing hid and go seek. I knew my bed was safe. I laid there while my leg was throbbing and heard the sounds of Normal childhood outside my window. I imagined myself outside with them and eventually I fell asleep praying that I wouldn't be awoken for one of Moms "talks" in the middle of the night.

My mattress was a very old, used, twin spring mattress and the springs were popping out which made it hard to sleep on it. I never had a comfortable place to lay my legs because the springs would scratch them if I moved the wrong way.

School started up again and Dad was really good about getting me a pair of new shoes, a few sweaters and 2 skirts and tights to start the year off. My favorite thing to get was a new lunch pail and umbrella. It always came in handy on a rainy day in Seattle, walking to school in my red goulashes over my new shoes to keep them dry.

## SECRETS BEHIND THE FOUR WALLS
and the Monster Mother That Lived Inside Them

Entering the 3rd grade I was a good student. I loved my teacher because she treated me with such kindness. She was great at finding my attributes and learning abilities to work at our own pace. Miss Cooper's birthday was coming up so I wanted to do something nice for her. I walked to Bartells Drug Store and with some change I had saved up I bought her a rain bonnet. Back in those days women wore "plastic rain bonnets" so their hair wouldn't get wet or messed up by the wind. I had just enough...1 dollar and some change. I took the small, brown bag and walked the 2 miles home. I was excited to give Miss Copper her gift the next day when I got to school.

When I made it home I proceeded to wrap the bonnet up complete with a bow on top. I handed the wrapped present to Miss Cooper and she looked so pleased saying "thank you Rani, I will get a lot of good use out this bonnet." Seeing how happy it made Miss. Cooper made me feel great. I walked home that Friday afternoon and Mom picked me up from the house. It was her payday and our routine was to go fill her tank with gas, stop at the liquor store to buy her bourbon then head home.

That night mom started drinking and I went to bed. She stayed up drinking, talking to one of her friends on the phone. Around 3 AM she stormed in my room because after counting her bow collection she realized that one was missing and she ordered me to look for it. She had a large box of bows that she bought and made, kept in a storage room with other wrapping paper, paint outdoor furniture and yard tools. There were around 500 used and new bows in this box. She had to of sat there and counted the entire box of bows to realize that one particular one was missing. Looking back I think she deliberately went looking for a reason to yank or drag me out bed that night.

Mom yelled "I'm missing one of my bows!" "It's my special bow!" There was no way she could have noticed that one little bow was missing out of the hundreds that she kept in this box. She pushed me into the room and told me I had better find it or else. I had no idea what I was looking for I just dumped the big box on the floor and started looking for her one "special bow".

A half hour later she flung open the storage room door holding a huge stick that she used to beat David and I. In a very evil tone she asked "did you find it yet?" Knowing there was no way I was going to find this bow, she just wanted a reason to torment me that night. While yelling "You better find it" she hit me very hard with the huge stick right on the top of my head splitting it wide open. I didn't know I was

## Secrets Behind the Four Walls
### and the Monster Mother That Lived Inside Them

bleeding and continued looking for this imaginary bow. I found one that did look sort of fancy so I set it aside to show Mom.

Just as I was starting to put the bows back she flung open the door again and asked "have you found it yet." I told her in a very soft voice that I think so and as I looked down I noticed there was a puddle of "red stuff" beneath me. I looked up at mom and said "I think I spilled some red paint." Dad had a can of red paint in there that he had used to paint my tricycle a few years back. Mom got a look on her face of anger and told me to clean it up. After I cleaned the mess I realized the "red stuff" was coming from my head. It was blood. Mom had me get in the bathtub and she started rinsing my head with ice cold water and it started to really hurt. When she was done she had me dry off and get to bed. I did. She kept me out school the next day and had me stay in my bed which I did.

Not all was bad all the time, she was at times a very loving and giving person. She had 2 very close friends that she had for years and her co-workers loved her. The best time I had spent with my mom was when we would take a trip to Yakima in the summer time for a small vacation. Mom would call dad and ask him for a little money so we could take the long, road trip to Eastern Washington and stay in the Travel

# Rani

Lodge Hotel. Dad would buy flotation mattresses for mom and I and we always had the best time.

Mom didn't swim but I did all day from sun up to sun down. I was free to play and make friends. Mom drank but not as heavily as she did at home. Mom had a great time also. Sometimes we would walk to the mall and do some shopping. Those were the best times and the memories I try to hang on to. It would quickly come to an end and back home we went where the heavy drinking and abuse would resume.

What still haunts me to this day is that I can only remember one birthday party Mom threw for me when I was around 8-9. David had come up from Centralia which must have been a surprise to Mom because she put together a small party very quickly and very late, around 7pm that night. She had me run around and ask some neighborhood kids to come over. I was so happy

The only birthday party I ever remember having

## Secrets Behind the Four Walls
### and the Monster Mother That Lived Inside Them

to see David. Dad dropped him off and he was holding a gift for me. It was a Barbie doll. I loved it so much I played with it all the time and took it everywhere with me.

Dad picked David up around an hour later and he was gone again. I missed him so much but even as young as I was I could tell David was uncomfortable at the house. I guess he hated being there. He was there for my birthday and that meant a lot to me. I didn't want him to leave ever.

This is the Barbie David gave me. I'm pictured here with my mum.

There was a point in my home where it seemed things were a little better. Mom was having relations with a married man who lived right across the street from our house were his wife and 2 sons lived.

The sons were my age and close friends of mine. Mom really liked him and wanted to paint this picture for him that our house was a perfect home. It was a very crazy situation. Dan (the man) would sleep over

# Rani

at our house then walk across the street to his house the next day. His wife Honey moved out and stayed with her sister. The 2 boys stayed with Dan at their house.

Honey would drive up and down our street, have her sisters threaten my Mom and park on the hill behind the hill of our house and watch it for hours and hours. Trying to see what her husband was doing with my Mom.

Around this time Moms boyfriend Ron found out about the relationship with Dan. He came to our house one Saturday night while David was staying over for the weekend. While asleep in my room David and I were awoken up by Mom and Ron arguing so loud I thought the whole neighborhood could hear them. David sat on the bed with me while Mom ran down the hall into her room. Ron caught her and punched her so hard that she fell onto the bed backwards.

He was sitting on top of her punching her so hard in the face that she almost bit her tongue in half. David and I were peeking through the crack in my bedroom door into Moms room where she was screaming for her life and bleeding out of her nose and mouth. She got away from Ron and locked herself in the bathroom. Later we found out the fight was not over the affair between Mom and Dan but over the fact Mom

## SECRETS BEHIND THE FOUR WALLS
### and the Monster Mother That Lived Inside Them

would not sign the car title to her 1965 Thunderbird over to him. Ron went and sat on the couch in the living room. David told me he was going to make Ron leave. David was around 13 and very tall. David found a mop stick in the kitchen and went in the living room yelling "Ron, you better leave!" Ron refused and David went to hit Ron in the head. He missed but scared Ron just enough that he quickly left the house that night.

After David locked all the doors and secured the windows in the house, he shut the lights off and we went to bed while Mom was locked in her bedroom severely beaten and bruised. Mom finally fell asleep as well. The next morning David and I were set to stay in Centralia for Spring break with our grandparents. Mom looked horrible. Her face and eyes were black and blue, her nose was broken and her tongue had been split open

This is the Thunderbird Ron beat my mum up for.

# Rani

on both sides. Dad was on his way to pick us up and take us to the train station. Mom made us promise not to tell Dad or let him in her bedroom. She didn't want Dad seeing her that way all swollen, black and blue. She was almost unrecognizable. I remember feeling so bad for her but relieved to get away.

When Dad came he wanted to talk to Mom but we told him she was still sleeping. That wasn't unusual for Mom so he didn't press the issue. Dad just said make sure to call her while we're down there. I had a great time that Spring Break. The only time I felt the "Normal" feeling. The time came to say my good byes to my grandparents and David and I took the long train ride home.

This is David and I standing with my Grandfather at his home. This was after Mike beat my mum the night befor

Mom was at the train station when I arrived looking beautiful as ever even though she was still swollen and a little black and blue around her eyes. She

## Secrets Behind the Four Walls
### and the Monster Mother That Lived Inside Them

stayed sober that week and she looked good. She was loving, caring and happy to me. Unfortunately, Mike came back a week later and apologized and ended up stayed with Mom for the next 10 years. Ron never beat mom again. He still came into my room naked at night, peaked at me through the hole in the wall, drank with Mom and cheated on her all of the time.

Ron found a lady friend that I think he really liked. Mom found out and she was furious. When she couldn't get ahold of Ron one night she piled me into the car and we drove over to his grandparents' house where Ron lived. Mom brought a bottle of wine with her and drank most of it on the way there. By the time we got there she was extremely drunk and I was embarrassed for her. Of course Ron was not home but his grandparents were.

Ron and my mum

Ron's grandma called me out of the car so I could try and calm Mom down. Grams as I use to call her

# Rani

told Mom she was the only woman Ron would ever love. After a while we left. Mom started driving home but the wine had made her sick so she pulled the car over and made me drive. It was very late at night and I was only in the 4$^{th}$ grade. I climbed in the drivers' seat, barely able to touch the petals or see out of the window and I set off home. Mom kept repeating over and over, "just get me home, just get me home!" Then she threw up. I only drove a short distance and after she threw up all over the car she drove the rest of the way home. She managed to run into a persons' front yard and over their rockery. Only with Gods guidance did we make it home in one piece. Mom made me clean up the vomit in the car before I could go to bed.

After time went on it seemed as those Mike and Mom had their own understanding they would stay together but also see other people. They weren't only addicted to alcohol and drugs but also addicted to each other. Moms drinking and the mere pleasure of abusing me never stopped and I was in living hell. Dad did everything that he could at that time with what he knew to help me. Back then there really were no resources for abused and neglected children. No websites to refer to or internet to search.

During this time Dad had purchased a beautiful home in Federal Way and owned a very successful

## SECRETS BEHIND THE FOUR WALLS
### and the Monster Mother That Lived Inside Them

directory business in Burien. Lynn moved into the house with Dad and shortly thereafter became pregnant. Dad was unhappy and thought she was trying to trap him. Their relationship was getting rocky due to the fact David had moved in with them and Lynn didn't want Dad being close to David or I. We were his kids and we couldn't just disappear but that is what Lynn wanted and she had no problem showing it.

As long as David lived in Dads home which was purchased before he married Lynn he was mistreated by Lynn. She treated him as though he was a second class citizen and not welcome there. Needless to say he went through a lot of problems while living there. Dad was working all the time and was rarely home. David was there with Lynn most days and nights alone. He was not allowed to go into the kitchen or upstairs when no one was home. He was not allowed to go in the refrigerator to get anything to eat. He was never given a key so he could get in the house after school or allowed to have friends over. He was very unhappy living there and started drinking himself. Due to the heavy drinking he crashed a car while living at Dads.

David was never treated right at home with mom and now he was being treated as a dog at Dads house with Lynn. I feel that David felt his real family was in Centralia with our grandparents. When he lived there

# Rani

he was doing well in school, he had lots of friends in school and was very close to the Lord. When he had to move in with Dad and Lynn he never felt as though he belonged. I always felt Dad had the worse luck with picking women. He couldn't have chosen 2 of the most defective women on the planet. Our mom Shelly and "to be" stepmom Lynn. I was 14 when Lynn became pregnant. Dad being in his late 40s was not happy though Lynn was thrilled. Lynn was quite a few years younger than Dad. He always felt she got pregnant because he wanted to leave the relationship.

Dad and Lynn got married with the Justice of the Peace while she was pregnant. Dad must have felt this was the right thing to do. Around 1979 Lynn gave birth to my half-brother Sam. I never seen Lynn the whole 9 months of her pregnancy nor was I invited to the hospital after his birth. I didn't even get a phone call the day Sam was born. I found out the birth and gender of the baby only because Mom drove me to Lynns moms dress shop in West Seattle. Lynn had a huge banner on the front of the store announcing "IT"S A BABY BOY!"

One week later, Dad called me and said they had had a baby and it was a boy. I was so mad at Dad. He had no idea that I already knew about the baby. David had already told me the news a few days earlier.

## Secrets Behind the Four Walls
### and the Monster Mother That Lived Inside Them

Needless to say the "Golden Child" was born. From that time on it was all about Sam. David and I took a backseat in Dads life. Shortly thereafter David married his high school sweetheart and moved out from Dads house.

David was finally free and happy. He had his own apartment and a beautiful, new wife. Dad convinced Lynn to let me move into his home which caused a lot of problems for Dad. Lynn didn't want dad to have any kind of a relationship with David or I. She wanted Dad all to herself and wanted him to forget that he ever had a life before her and their son Sam. The truth is Dad had a whole life before Lynn and Sam came along. He was a great father to David and I for a very long time. He loved us and we loved him.

Dad won the fight and I was able to move in. Dad was so happy that he was able to rescue me from the hell I lived in with Mom. I moved in and Lynn tried to be nice though she gave me the same rules David had. Stay downstairs, no friends over and don't touch anything. Dad enrolled me in Federal Way high school and got us a membership to the community pool where every Tuesday and Thursday we would go to swim. Dad also got me a job at the McDonalds in Burien near his work. I would work there on the weekends. I remember taking the bus really early in the morning to make

# Rani

it there right before they opened. I was also taking a Ballet class once a week. Lynn actually bought me a pink leotard and ballet shoes which surprised me. It was a pretty good life for a while.

Lynn gave me a lot of freedom. I had a boyfriend at this time that my mom was trying very hard to marry me off to. Jim was much older than I was and I knew he was too old for me. I think he must have been in his early 20s and was going to medical school. I was maybe 15 at the time. Jim expected me to act like a woman and he wanted to make me one. I avoided any contact with him like the plague.

I really liked my new boyfriend Giovanni. He was fun, my age and came from a large, welcoming Italian family. Giovanni would pick me up and we would go to Seattle Center, China Town and all the family get-togethers at his parents' house. Giovanni had a mom, dad, 3 sisters and a younger brother all living together in a nice house as a family. Around 6 months of dating I did the unthinkable and lost my virginity and got pregnant all in the same night. I was not ashamed as much as I was scared. I was so young. I was scared to tell Dad because he was so proud of me and we were becoming so close.

After a few weeks of trying to figure out what I was going to do, I decided to leave Dads home and

## Secrets Behind the Four Walls
### and the Monster Mother That Lived Inside Them

head back to Moms. Mom was happy only because she wanted Lynn and Dad to think they had failed. I woke up very early in the morning, packed my stuff and moved out without telling Dad. I took a bus back to Moms house. Dad called me hurt and confused as to why I had left. I had never heard that tone in Dads voice before. He wanted me to come back but I knew I couldn't.

Lynn was fine with me moving back to moms of course. She hated the time Dad and I spent together. After I moved out, it became all about the "Golden Child" Sam. Dad didn't want to fail a third time and really worked hard at being there for his son. Sam had a beautiful home; got everything he wanted and was never allowed to cry. It was all about making the perfect family and perfect kid.

I pulled away from Dad at this time; I couldn't understand the "Perfect Family" thing and didn't have much to do with him for a very long time. I was back in school, though there was one small problem. My growing tummy! Mom came to me late one night and asked me flat out "Rani, are you pregnant?" I said reluctantly "Yes." Her reaction was to slap me so hard in the face it knocked me off my feet. The next evening with a bottle of Bourbon at her bed she started calling everyone she knew including my dad. The humiliating Rani wheels were in motion. She even called an old childhood friend who had moved away and informed him of the abomination. Mom kicked me out of the house that night; I was 5 months pregnant scared and helpless.

Giovanni picked me up and we had to tell his mom. She understandably unhappy to hear I was pregnant but tried the best she could to comfort me. Giovanni on the other hand was excited. Mom called me at Giovannis parents' house saying that Dad wanted to talk to me. I certainly didn't want to talk to my dad; he had a new life which was fine with me. David called too and wanted me to meet him as well. During this time I was not close to David either but agreed to meet Him alone at Moms house. I got to Moms house and David wanted to talk to me alone without Mom present. Mom was reluctant but allowed us the privacy.

David started off by saying "I have some bad news; Dad has 5 stomach ulcers and probably wouldn't live another 5 years." All I remember saying was "good, I hope he dies." He asked if I would just talk to Dad for him, I agreed. Dad called and asked if he could pick me up and go for a ride and talk. We went to Saltwater Park and sat on a log by the beach and talked. He started off by saying "I love you more than anything, please let me help you. Dad said that mom had

# SECRETS BEHIND THE FOUR WALLS
## and the Monster Mother That Lived Inside Them

arranged for me to have an abortion and he was going to pay for it.

Giovanni 17
Me 16

I remember clearly how this made me feel. My first feeling was "Wow, Really?" Mom never took care of anything of importance for me, whether it was open houses at school or the spelling bee I won in 5$^{th}$ grade. This gave me a strange feeling in my stomach. Wow, my parents wanting to work together after 10 years of showing nothing but hatred for one another. All this unity just for the sake of killing the growing miracle in my stomach was beyond hurtful and disgusting. For one thing, I could feel the baby moving in my stomach, two, I already loved it with all my heart and three, I

# Rani

knew Giovanni would be heartbroken if I went along with what I call a forced abortion.

I was so very young, scared and not ready for a baby. I felt dizzy and in some kind of daze. I was so very confused. I really don't remember my response just that Dad and I went for ice cream. When he dropped me off, he came in Moms house and seeing Mom and Dad together made me sad. I never wanted them to get a divorce. For a moment my childhood feelings of "dad please don't leave me" came rushing back briefly just for a moment then quickly back to anger and despair I went. The two of them were telling me this was the only decision and I had no choice it was happening and arranged to be done in two days. I just stood there numb.

Dad kissed me good bye and told Mom he would call her later. Mom would not let me leave the house in fear I would run away. 2 days passed and I was picked up at the house by a friend of the family, not even my parents. The friend of the family took me to the abortion clinic, let me out of the car to walk in all by myself and waited for me while I had the abortion. What came next was the worse and most painful event ever. They laid me down on a stiff bed, in a cold room with very little words spoken. Only that "this is going to hurt a little." That was an understatement.

## Secrets Behind the Four Walls
### and the Monster Mother That Lived Inside Them

They started the first step which was to kill the fetus. I'm not sure what they did only that it hurt badly. I cried out. Afterwards I was sent home, confused and in pain. In no time at all I started cramping and spotting blood. I had to go back in a few days for what they called the second half of the "late term" abortion procedure I was forced to get. Once again believe it or not the same family friend, not my mom or dad, drove me again to the abortion clinic. I was laid down on a hard bed in a cold room, my legs placed in stirrups, and with no explanation of what was to come, the nurse just told me to relax as she held my legs open. I was shaking uncontrollably and terrified. The doctor said "We are going to place 3 seaweed sticks in to dilate your cervix." It hurt so bad I wanted to scream. He said I would feel some discomfort but that I had to relax. With all the tremendous pain I was in it was very hard to "relax."

Afterwards the doctor was explained to me that I would have some cramping, spotting and quit possibly lose the baby at home. I was due to go back in 2 more days. Once again I was driven by the family friend to the abortion clinic, taken back to the cold, dark room and the painful procedure was performed once again. He explained that I would again have cramping and bleedings and could lose the fetus at home. Off I went

# Rani

scared to death that while being home alone I would lose the baby I still had inside me. There is no way possible to describe the pain or incredible fear I felt not knowing if the baby was going to just fall out dead and I would be all alone.

The next few days were horrible. I had severe cramping and was very lightheaded and dizzy not to mention scared to death. A few days later I was taken in to a different room where a large machine stood with a large hose. The nurse came in and got me ready for what was to come. The Doctor came in and asked how I was feeling. I told him I was cramping and bleeding a little bit. I was instructed to lie back and put my feet in the stirrups. The doctor stated that after this last procedure I would no longer be pregnant as if I was supposed to be happy .

The Doctor sat down in front of me, while the nurse held my legs apart as they shook violently. I was so cold and scared out of my mind and all the nurse could say was hold still and relax. What I heard next sounded like a freight train coming through the room. It was a vacuum machine specially developed for abortion. The loud sound of the machine stopped and it seemed to me the doctor was pulling and tugging something out of me. Piece by piece, I felt it all! Every tug and every pull. Then again the freight train

## Secrets Behind the Four Walls
### and the Monster Mother That Lived Inside Them

started sucking my baby out piece by piece tarring it to shreds. When the abortion was over I was informed that I was no longer pregnant. The doctor asked if I wanted to know the sex, I said "yes." It was a little girl. I never wanted the abortion in the first place and now it was over. My baby girl ripped from me from the inside out.

All the hiding and all the pain was over. I knew Giovanni was going to be devastated. He pleaded for this not to happen but I was given no choice. The next few weeks went by and I was kept out of school and put on antibiotics to prevent infection. I was not allowed to see Giovanni and I was severely depressed. I wanted my baby girl back. Four weeks past and David came over to Moms to see how I was doing and then we went to dinner. Giovanni was even allowed to come to dinner with us.

David was not happy that Giovanni was coming because he felt he wasn't there for me during the abortion. When he got to Moms house David slammed him up against the wall and was yelling "where were you when Rani needed you?" "You couldn't call her or see how she was doing?" David was so angry and it was the first time he ever showed me that he cared for me and was worried about me. Everything calmed down and we went to Black Angus for dinner. It was Moms birthday.

# Rani

This is the picture I took of David driving us
back from the resterant that night

    We all sat down and immediately Mom ordered a Double Pina Colada. The food came and so did another Pina Colada for Mom. Dessert came and so did another double Pina Colada. Mom got very drunk so we paid the bill and left the restaurant. We got in the car, Daviddrove and Mom sat in front. Giovanni and I sat in the back. For the most part the drive was quiet. Mom kept turning around and giving me dirty looks. She did this more than once; I hadn't done anything to make her mad. Mom was drunk and I was always her target.

    David took notice and said Mom "why in the hell are you looking at Rani like that?" Mom mumbled something then gave me even a dirtier look as if to say "you're going to get it when we get home!" I'm sure

## Secrets Behind the Four Walls
### and the Monster Mother That Lived Inside Them

she blamed me for David getting mad at her. We arrived home, mom got out of the car, slammed the door then slammed the house door behind her. Giovanni got in his car, said he would call me later and left. I was standing outside bagging David to take me with him and please let me live with him. As I had heard so many times in the past from Dad, David simply said "I can't Rani, I can't" I felt helpless and scared to enter the house. David said to call him if it got bad. I stood there scared to go inside. I felt I had no one and no way out.

I went inside the house where I was met with a stick to my head. I fell to the floor and tried to protect myself as Mom was yelling "thanks for ruining my birthday dinner", "you're a whore" and "thanks a lot for making David mad at me!" Mom yelled for me to get in my room and then she pulled my phone from the wall that Dad had given me. Mom proceeded to get drunk and call my grandparents with the news of I ruined her birthday dinner and what a whore I was and how I need God in my life.

About a month or so later my friend and I got into our minds that we wanted to go to a private school. We would ride the bus downtown to an alternative school and hung out. We really thought this school was for us. I called Dad and told him I wanted to go to this alternative school. Dad informed me there was no structure at the alternative school but that he would consider a private school. I found an all-girls private catholic school called Holy Names. Holy Names Academy was very expensive and hard to get accepted into. I had to take an entry level test to see if I qualified to enroll. I passed and started there in the Fall. I had to get up 2 hours early to take the long bus ride to school each morning. I loved attending Holy Names Academy and I made new friends. I tried out for the Cheer Team and made it. I was so proud of myself and for the first time in a long time I was happy. The Catholic school was run by very strict nuns but I didn't mind. I loved my classes and loved the school.

Finally I felt that everyone was proud of me and for the first time I felt proud of myself. Dad provided everything I needed to make this all work. New clothes, lunch money and a bus pass. I know he did all this because he wanted me to succeed in life and for me to be happy. I was and doing very well. I could never move forward from the loss of my baby girl in the late term abortion I was forced to get. I tried moving forward and pretending it never happened but would find myself obsessing over and over it.

I was still seeing Giovanni against my families' wishes. I felt safe with him. Not sure that I loved him but loved the freedom he seemed to have. Giovanni would pick me up after school at Holy Names and we started having an intimate relationship again. I came up with what I thought was a solution for all my suffering due to the loss of my little girl. I told Giovanni I wanted my baby back. I needed to fill the void I had in my heart. Needless to say I became pregnant again while attending Holy Names Academy. Once again, I tried to hide my pregnancy even harder now from my mom and everyone else.

I started to show and the nuns took notice of my growing belly. I was called out of class and sent to the head nuns office where 3 nuns sat waiting. They asked if I was pregnant. My response was "Yes I am." They informed me that I could no longer attend Holy Names Academy and I was told to leave. I was worried about Dads reaction to this news and in my mind I knew I was about to let him down once again. I walked to the telephone booth nearby and called Giovanni. He picked me up and we went to his parents' house to discuss what was going to happen next. All Giovanni could say was "please don't go back home!" He was so afraid that my parents were going to make me have another abortion. I certainly didn't want that.

We waited for his Mom Guisipina to come home from work. Giovanni and his mom went into her

# Rani

bedroom and shortly after she called me in as well. She asked me if I was pregnant and I said "Yes!" She told us that we can't have this baby because were too young. She offered me 250.00 to have an abortion. Giovanni ran out of the room calling for me to follow. He said were leaving and staying away. I'm not sure where he thought we were going but he just wanted us to get out of that house quickly.

Guisipina said "Ok we will deal with this" not wanting us to leave. I moved in to his parents' house and got a job in Burien at a sandwich shop. Dad was there for me. He would come to my work and have lunch. Giovannis older sister Phillis helped me get on Public Assistance. Dad helped me get into a very nice apartment and helped furnish the place nicely. Giovanni didn't live with me but the closer I got to giving birth the more he stayed over at my apartment.

The blessed time came.. I woke Giovanni up around 1AM and we called my doctor. He told us to get to the hospital. I was scared so I told Giovanni to take me to his moms house instead. Giovanni and I woke up the whole house and they were telling me I better get to the hospital but I could only say "I want to go later!" The labor pains were coming fast and I could wait no longer so off we went. Around 545AM on May 11th 1983 I gave birth to a 9lb 5oz Baby Girl.

## SECRETS BEHIND THE FOUR WALLS
### and the Monster Mother That Lived Inside Them

I fell in love instantly. She was the most beautiful baby I've ever seen with chubby red cheeks, puffy little lips and biggest brown eyes I have seen.

Dad came to the hospital and made sure I had the best private room, with a tv. He wanted everything to be perfect. In those days you stayed in the hospital for 4 or 5 days. Mom came and brought a gift and left. I was released a few days later with my new baby girl. I was 17 years old. In years to come Giovanni and I struggled with our relationship.

I felt he should be more responsible and he still wanted to be a teenager. My life was finally complete with my little angel Tiffany Rochelle. About 3 months later I enrolled in Seattle Community College and received my GED. Shortly after I started Beauty School in Burien. I wanted to move from my one bedroom apartment into a two bedroom apartment so

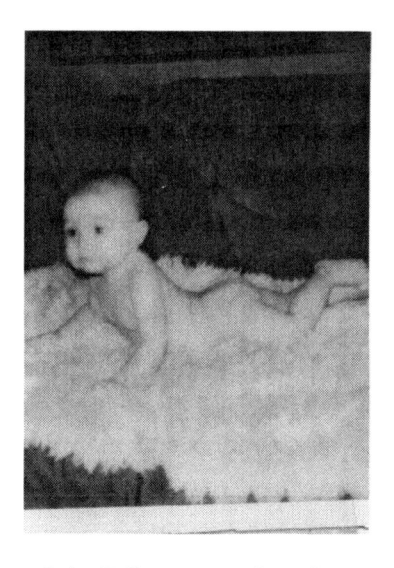

Baby Tiffany, my Pride and Joy

# Rani

my baby and I moved back in with my mom so I could save up some money for the deposit and first months rent.

While Tiffany and I were staying at moms house Ron would come over and stay the night. One morning while Mom and I were cooking breakfast we caught Mike walking into my bedroom where Tiffany was sleeping in her crib. Ron was completely naked as usual. Mom yelled "Ron what the hell are you doing?" I looked at mom and said "see, I told you!!" Mom kicked Ron out and that was the end of their 11 year relationship. I was glad.

Mom fell into her alcoholism even more. Ron was a companion for her and now it was gone and she had no one. I was a mother myself now and moving on with my life. Mike was no longer a part of Moms life, she had no relationship with David and I had my own life. She only had a few friends she would drunk call every now and then. Alcohol was truly the demise of my Mom Rochelle Lee. In 1986 my life took a dramatic change.

I moved out of moms house, was going to beauty school and due to moms drinking being so out of control I did not let her see my daughter Tiffany. I was working as a receptionist at a hair salon and hadn't talked to Mom in close to 3 weeks. I called her for a

## SECRETS BEHIND THE FOUR WALLS
### and the Monster Mother That Lived Inside Them

few days but couldn't get a hold of her. I took Tiffany to Giovannis parents' house and drove over to Moms. I could have never imagined what I was about to find.

There were 3 Sunday newspapers on the front porch and the whole house was closed up. There was no answer at the door. The worse feeling came over me so I left. I raced back to Giovannis parents and told him something is really wrong over at moms. I called my Brother and told him "I think something is wrong with Mom!" He replied panicked "What?" I said I didn't know. I explained what I had seen and asked if he would meet me over there. He said "of course!" We arrived at this same time. I was pounding on the door and David was pounding on Moms bedroom window. We got no response.

We both went into panic mode and David started removing one of the bedroom window screens so we could get in the house. We must have scared Mom because the front door opened and she asked us "What are you doing?" What I saw horrified me to the bone. She was standing there with yellow eyes and yellow skin. I looked at David and yelled for him to call an ambulance. Mom was trying to act like she was ok but we both knew better. We all went in the house, it was all closed up. It was the middle of the afternoon and the house was dark and dingy inside. David

# RANI

was calling for an ambulance to get there quick. Mom asked for a glass of ice water.

I went in the kitchen and I looked in the fridge to find only pickle juice and moldy spaghetti. It was obvious that she had been drinking the pickle juice and not eating. It was February and the eerie thing was Mom still had her Christmas tree up that I bought for her and decorated together. There were still presents under the tree unwrapped. The house smelled awful. Unlike anything I had ever smelled before. The smell was of vomit, feces and old blood, lots of blood.

I told Mom we were going to take her to the hospital. She didn't want to go, she simply wanted to go back to bed. I informed that we were going to take her whether she wanted to or not. I think that's when she surrendered. I went down the hall to her bedroom to get her some clean clothes and what I saw was truly a scene from a horror movie. I yelled for David. What we saw was unimaginable. Why she would not have cried out for help to this day I still don't understand! Instead Mom unplugged her phone and practically let herself bleed to death. Her bed was blood soaked, the bedding and carpet was blood soaked and there was blood splatters all over the walls as if someone had been shot with a shotgun. There was a blood soaked

# SECRETS BEHIND THE FOUR WALLS
### and the Monster Mother That Lived Inside Them

trail on the floor from her bed to the hall and into the bathroom where the scene was even more gruesome.

The bathroom had blood splatters everywhere. The walls, the sink, the mirror but the toilet was the worst. The toilet was full of thick, black stuff clear to the top almost overflowing. To this day I still don't know what that was, blood clots, millions of them, or black fesses, maybe both? I don't really know. I didn't get a chance to change. I later seen that while we were outside knocking on the door Mom had changed from her blood soaked nightgown into the one she was wearing when she answered the door. She tried very hard hide what must have been an enormous amount of agony. All she kept saying when we were there was that she was so thirsty. Giovanni was sitting on the couch next to her trying to make small talk. The ambulance came and took Mom to the hospital. I stayed behind at the house and wanted to try and clean up the mess. I called Dad and told him to come to Moms fast. I could tell in his voice he knew it was going to be bad.

I started to open the house up. It was a crisp, sunny February morning. I opened the windows and let some light and fresh air in. David followed the ambulance to the West Seattle Hospital. Dad arrived and I took him down the hall to the bedroom and then into the bathroom. He couldn't believe she lived through that. All

Dad could say was "what in the hell happened here?!" Dad looked around, he looked in the fridge and cupboards. He took notice that the Christmas tree was still up. He said "how are we ever going to clean this all up?" I said that Giovanni and myself would do it all though I had no idea how or where to start.

On Dads way out he turned to me and said "we need to get her help" I said "I know Dad, I know!" He told me he would do whatever it takes. He would take care of everything and to make sure she gets whatever she needs. He said to make sure I called my grandparents in Centralia. A few days later Grandma showed up, Grandpa did not. Grandma never went to see Mom in the hospital, she just stayed at the house taking care of unpaid bills, bounced checks and going through pictures and household items.

Grandma left and went back to Centralia without saying good bye to her daughter. I went to see Mom in the hospital. She was in the ICU. She had tubes coming out of her mouth and nose. They were there to suck the bile out of her stomach that was so big and bloated it looked like she was 9 months pregnant. She still was very yellow. Her poisoned blood the color of mustard was coming out in one bag and new blood was being transfused into Mom through IV trying to give her a second chance at life. Her liver was so hard that her body was not filtering or keeping in the new blood.

As the doctor explained to me, her liver had hardened like driftwood. The liver acts as a filter and due to the Cirrhosis, her liver would not filter the blood and it was spitting out of her body. A few days later she was moved out of ICU into a private room. At this point I still had hope for her recovery. Grandma had left me some money to buy Mom a nice nightgown, robe and slippers for her stay in the hospital so she would feel better. I took them up the hospital and she was very happy to receive these things.

Mom said that she felt kind of icky. She wanted the tubes out and she wanted to take a bath believe it or not. I think she was starting to feel better. Her stomach still looked as if she was 9 months pregnant and she was still very yellow. I joked around with Mom a little and asked if she was pregnant and if she needed to tell me something. Mom struggled some and gave me a little giggle saying "I don't think so!" I laughed then had to leave.

The next morning Dad called and said he wanted to see Mom. I made sure to get there before him so I could let mom knew Dad was coming to see her. Mom immediately was concerned with now she looked. She wanted her new robe and lipstick from her purse. I

# Rani

made her look as good as I could with all the tubes coming out of her. They still hadn't bathed her so I brushed her hair away from her face (still having blood in it) and pinned it into a bun.

She was such a beautiful woman, when I say beautiful I mean stunning. She looked just like Elizabeth Taylor though in my eyes a more beautiful version. She was small and petite with stunning features. She had strikingly blue eyes with long black lashes. A very exotic nose, beautiful mouth and voice to match. Still as she lay there in the hospital bed, hooked up, yellow from the jaundice, bloated from the Cirrhosis of her liver she still just looked beautifully stunning!

I put the pink robe on her and gave her pink lipstick she always wore. She applied the lipstick, looked up at me and asked "how do I look?" I said "you look great, and Dad should be here soon." Dad arrived at the hospital and as we walked towards her hospital room I tried to explain how she looked. I told Dad she was very yellow and extremely bloated but in good spirits. Dad entered the room and a very shocked look came over his face and tears welled up in his eyes. Mom looked over and held out her hand to Dad with the IV needle in place. She said in a very petite low voice "Hi Rick!" Dad replied "well Hello Shelly." I

# Secrets Behind the Four Walls
## and the Monster Mother That Lived Inside Them

could tell Dad was shaking with a horrified look in his face that he was trying to hide.

He sat in a chair beside moms' bed holding her hand. They were looking at each other with such love. It was very obvious they were still very much in love with each other. Dad asked how she was and she replied that she was doing fine but that she just needed to get better and that she wanted to go home. Dad said "I know Shelly." The doctor came in the room asking to speak to me. The Doctor and I took the elevator down to the next floor into the lobby area. I didn't want to sit so the doctor got right to the point. He said Moms liver was too far gone and there was no chance of it repairing itself.

I asked what we needed to do. He said she could be put on a list for a Liver transplant but that he was unsure if she would make it long enough to receive one. He also informed me that the hospital was not equipped to care for all her medical needs. I asked if she could be transferred to Harborview because I knew it was the best hospital in the State known for its trauma center and ground breaking medicine.

I asked if he would stay on board to oversee Moms care and he said of course he would. He felt she was too weak and ill for the transport to Harborview but if I decided to do this it would have to be done quickly

# RANI

because her kidneys and pancreas were starting to fail. As the doctor and I were finishing our conversation Dad came walking into the lobby looking as though he has just been crying. The doctor told me to call him the next day with my decision and he left.

Dad came up and asked what the doctor had said. I informed him there was nothing more this hospital could do for Mom and told him I was working on transferring Mom right away to Harborview Hospital. This was a big responsibility for a 20 year old. Dad started on a game plan for Mom should she recover and go home. He wanted to put her in the best recovery center the state had to offer, sell her house and get her a condo. Dad was determined to do anything and everything to get the help Mom needed to free her from alcoholism and stress. For her to have a better chance at a new life. He gave me a big hug and kiss and said he would take care of everything including all her medical bills that she would acquire.

I went back to Moms room. She was out of her bed, sitting on a portable toilet and they were trying to get her to have a bowel movement. Her body was in convulsions and I could tell she was in so much pain. She looked so small, helpless and hunched over almost childlike at that moment. Seeing Mom like this was breaking my heart! I could tell by the look in her eyes

## SECRETS BEHIND THE FOUR WALLS
### and the Monster Mother That Lived Inside Them

that she was scared. I went and found a nurse and asked if they could bath her. They assured me they could but that it would only be a sponge bath.

I asked if they could wash her hair, and they told me they would arrange it. The nurse informed me that the doctor ordered mom to eat a small amount of food. One poached egg and some apple juice. They got her all cleaned up and into a freshly changed bed. They brought her food and she ate it. After a while she said she was still hungry. David arrived and asked mom how she was doing and she told him she was hungry. She didn't like the bland poached egg so David asked her what she felt like eating. She stated she wanted McDonalds but that she knew the "grumpy old nurse" wouldn't let her have it. David said, don't worry we will sneak it in. Mom wanted French fries with lots of salt and a thick chocolate shake. We probably shouldn't have but shortly after Brother arrived back, food in hand and Moms eyes lit up.

David also picked up food for us and we all ate together with doors shut so no one could see. We all enjoyed our food especially mom. "Oh boy" she kept saying, "this is good!" She sure did enjoy her lunch that day. After we ate David asked "what should we sneak you for dinner mom?" She happily requested pork chops, with green beans and cream of mushroom soup with a Pepsi. We cleaned up all the evidence. Mom was tired so we let her rest and told her we would be back later.

Off to the store I went and I prepared her dinner at Giovannis parents' house. Later that night at visitation hour we removed the poached egg and apple juice replacing it with the pork chops, green beans and a large Pepsi. Her face lit up and with a big smile she started to eat. Very slowly she took one weak bite after another. Mom wasn't able to eat it all, just a very small portion of it. She did say afterwards that maybe she should stick to the poached egg and apple juice. We cleaned everything up and let her sleep.

David brought her his special blanket and covered her because she always said she was freezing cold. We all parted and went home. I went to my apartment, and the next morning I was up early, getting Tiffany dressed and fed. I took her over to her grandparents because I knew I had a lot of work ahead of me. I sat at the kitchen table pen and paper in hand and I was determined to get mom transferred to Harborview. I called and talked to a nurse explaining the situation how we needed to transfer mom to a facility that could meet her medical needs. She told me she would need to speak with the doctor overseeing Moms care so I gave his information to her.

# SECRETS BEHIND THE FOUR WALLS
## and the Monster Mother That Lived Inside Them

After they spoke with Moms Doctor they approved the transfer but not before informing me of all the risks. I thought surely at this point Mom had nothing to lose. She would die with or without the extreme care she needed so in my mind we had to take the risk. All they had to do was keep her stable in the ambulance ride for a half hour to Harbor View Hospital. Mom was set for the transfer the very next morning. I immediately went to the hospital to tell mom that we were transferring her to a better hospital. I arrived at her room she was resting. She was looking a lot. Her eyes and skin still yellow but not as bad. I asked the nurse if I could wash her hair and she said "sure." She brought me water, soap and a small sink and with the nurses help we washed Moms hair. After we were finished she said she felt so much better. When mom would talk she would stutter and had trouble getting her words out. This was due to the poison in her body attacking her brain. After the nurse finished changing her bedding she got back in bed and Mom and I had a very serious talk.

I took hold of her small frail hand and just held on for a minute or two. I asked Mom "do you know why you're here?" Her response was "because I am very sick." I asked if she knew why she was sick and she responded "yes." I asked "why?" She said she must have caught something from the elderly lady she was caring for. I told her in a very stern, low voice that she was in the hospital for drinking too much. Of course she said "No, I must have caught something from the elderly lady, she has been sick."

I was determined that Mom realize the harsh truth of why she was in the hospital. I told her she was in there because her liver had failed and her kidneys had shut down. I told her she was terminally ill from the years and years of drinking to much. In a very low, shaky voice she finally said "you're probably right." I said "the doctors told me most likely you're going to die." I asked her if she wanted to die. Mom replied this time in a clear voice "not if I can feel better." I told her she was going to be transferred to a better hospital that next day and she would receive all the care she needed to get better. She said "no I want to go home and be in my own bed." I told her she would be able to go home when she was healthier.

I let her know that David was coming to see her and she replied "He is?" with an ashamed tone in her voice. Before falling asleep she grabbed my hand and said "tell David I'm sorry!" My response was "what?" I couldn't believe what I was hearing. She repeated herself "tell David I'm sorry, ok!" I said that I would, covered her frail body and moved the poached egg that

## SECRETS BEHIND THE FOUR WALLS
### and the Monster Mother That Lived Inside Them

she refused to eat out of the way. I went home to my apartment and put my daughter Tiffany to bed then went to sleep myself. It was hard to fall asleep that night. I had so much on my mind with the decision to move Mom but I was still hopeful for her recovery. Giovanni was at my apartment with me for support and company. He had fallen asleep on the couch that night watching tv.

The phone rang around 345AM and it was my Brother David. Giovanni answered and gave the phone to me. David said the words I never wanted to hear. "Mom died!" I started screaming and crying. When I calmed down I asked him if he was at the hospital and he said yes that he was sitting on the bed with her. I asked if she looked peaceful or if there was a struggle and he told me she looked as though she had just fallen asleep. She was still covered in the blanket that David had brought her and she was finally at peace.

I found out, 15 years later David told me he never got on the elevator to see Mom. He was too scared to see her like that. I told David I was on my way to the hospital to see her as I was crying uncontrollably. He told me no and that he didn't want me to see her like that. He told me to call grandma and grandpa and I did. I was in total shock. I felt unbelievably lost.

I couldn't understand because we were supposed

to get her transferred and she was supposed to get better. We made all the necessary arrangements. I called Ron her ex-boyfriend of 11 years even though they had been broken up for several years. He broke down in disbelief. After making all the calls I felt lost and didn't know what to do next. Giovanni suggested that we head over to his parents' house in which we did. His mom met us at the door and she was so sad for me and the loss of my Mom. She tried comforting me and wanted to feed me though I wasn't hungry. She laid me on the couch with a blanket and gave me a Valium to relax my mind and broken heart.

Guisipina just sat there by my side. I fell asleep for a short while only waking a short period later still not believing that I had just lost my mom. I phoned my grandparents and they were already making the necessary arrangements. Grandma told me to head to the hospital for Moms belongings in which I did. Leaving the hospital with her things I just felt sick to my stomach. A feeling I will never forget nor can I describe.

I picked up Tiffany then headed home. Dad came over very upset and asked if we wanted to go to lunch. Still feeling like I was in the "Twilight Zone" we all got in Dads car and headed to the Country Kitchen, our favorite place to eat. Sitting in Dads car was the brochure for a Rehab Center and a "to do" list that included find a condo for Shelly. The ride to the restaurant was nothing but awkward small talk. Dad was mostly playing word games with Tiffany who was sitting in the backseat. I informed Dad that I had picked up Moms things. We didn't really say much else to each other. Dad mostly played with Tiffany as I sat there trying to wrap all my feelings and emotions around the loss of my Mom. After lunch we headed back to my apartment. That night I put Tiffany to bed then called Giovanni and talked to him for a while.

    I was having a very hard time falling asleep. Around 1am I finally dozed off. I wasn't in a deep sleep mostly tossing and turning. Around 3am my phone rang which wasn't uncommon because Giovanni was a night owl and use to call me very late at night all the time. As strange and unbelievable as this may sound, it really happened.

    The phone I had sitting on my floor by my bed, rang. It rang around 3-4 times. I rolled over, reached down and answered it. I said "Hello" On the other end of the phone was a voice that I could never even fathom hearing on the other end. It was my Mom, she said "Hi Honey!" With a pause and very shocked voice I replied "Mom?" I was so wide awake and shocked that I couldn't really put together what was going on. She replied "Yes!" I said "Mom you're dead!" and my voice was shaking. She said "what are you talking about?" Then I asked her if she wasn't dead then what year was it. To this day I don't understand what made me ask her that question but her response to this question still puzzles me. She said "it's 1972!" She was answering me like I was going crazy asking her such questions.

I was so freighted by that I hung up the phone and quickly felt a fear come over me that I have never felt before. I went in to my hall closet and grabbed the clothes she had worn while in hospital and all her stuff in the closet. The closet was filled with the stench of disease and death. A smell I will never forget. I grabbed her purse that had all her things in it and threw them all in a large, clear garbage bag, grabbed Tiffany and got the hell out of my apartment. I was so terrified that I drove to a park and ride where there was a donation drop box. I literally threw all her things out of my car window and sped off. I drove over to Giovanni's parents' house. It was very early in the morning.

I rang and rang the doorbell and Giovanni finally answered. All I could say was "MOM CALLED ME ON THE PHONE, MOM CALLED ME ON THE PHONE!" I woke his Mom up from my hysteria and she simply placed me on the couch and made some tea for me. After that day, I never spoke of this incident. Looking back now I wish I would have talked to her longer. She

## Secrets Behind the Four Walls
### and the Monster Mother That Lived Inside Them

was reaching out to me even after death and I hung up on her! Being a young woman of 20 I didn't know how to express it. From then on I looked for her in crowds, passing cars, and grocery cars. I looked and looked only wishing to see her face or hear her voice one more time. Only if I would have stayed on the phone, I never would have hung up!

From then on my life took a dramatic change. I was always sad. I constantly had a sick, gut wrenching feeling in my stomach that never really went away. I carried the fear that Mom was mad at me. I feared that constantly when she was alive and it carried into her death too. I was given the responsibility to clean out Moms house so I gave some furniture to Giovannis parents and sent important artwork and papers to my grandparents' house. I also held a large estate sale which was very hard. I had to go through all Moms things and get it ready to sale. I just knew this would make Mom mad.

She would have never liked people going through her house let alone her personal things. I would drive over to Moms house late at night after school even before I entered the home there was a sense that something was there and didn't want me there. I just shook it off as though it was all in my mind though now I'm

# Rani

not so sure it was. After 3 weeks we ended the garage sale and took the rest to the Salvation Army.

I decided to move Tiffany and I into Moms house which was ok with David and Dad as long as I paid the house payment. I worked and was going to school so Dad knew that wouldn't be a problem. Quickly I started fixing the house up. Trying to bring life and cheer to the dark and gloomy home. Giovanni and I panted the dark gray and gold walls white and I covered the dark wood paneling in flower wallpaper. I hung a crystal chandelier which brought light into this dim, dark home. Mom always had orange light bulbs in every lamp, in every room, that was one of the first things I changed so there could finally be bright light in the house.

Dad arranged for new carpet to be laid throughout the whole house. It was light beige which replaced the dirty olive green carpet. We also replaced the thick, dark green blackout curtains that kept the daylight out. I removed the foil from Moms bedroom and it was ready for all white blinds to be installed that were bought by Giovannis mom as a gift to me. The house was finally ready. It no longer smelled of blood, fesses' and death. It was a warm place and not cold had laughter not despair and anger. No matter what I did or change about the house there was always a feeling that something did not want you there. It was hard to shake it off.

This is where my drinking really started. I probably shouldn't have moved in there. While living there I found myself trying to relive things from my past. I hung out at the neighbor's house, contacted old friends and had them over at the house. I listened to all the music Mom used to play all while I was drinking, drinking and more drinking. I literally was turning into my mom. While living there I drove over the floating bridge from Bellevue to West Seattle at 2am in a black out and woke up with no recollection of how I got home. I got a DUI in the 1980s and had to go to a 2 day overnight alcohol class. Dad quickly put the house on the market. Thank God it sold fast.

I moved around a bit from Giovannis parents' house to one apartment to another. I found a small home for rent in Des Moines while working at a local grocery store. Around 1988 I became pregnant. I was ok with it though not elated. Giovanni and I sat down and talked about what we should do. We decided Marriage would be best. We had been together since 1981 and gone through a lot at our young age. Immediately we announced our engagement and set a date for 10/15/1988. I knew it would take time to

# RANI

plan the wedding and I didn't want a baby bump on my wedding day.

I made arrangement to marry at my childhood church. We held the reception just down the street. I made all the arrangement by myself and paid for the wedding with the money I received from the sale of Moms house. Giovannis mom made my wedding dress, and I made all the flower arrangements the bridesmaids would carry. I worked very long hours to make it a perfect wedding. I still felt uneasy marrying Giovanni. He was not a very good boyfriend. He drank and had a cocaine addiction. He hung out with losers and never financially helped me with Tiffany. I was determined to change all that when we got married.

Giovanni and I in the limo on our Wedding Day 1988

## Secrets Behind the Four Walls
### and the Monster Mother That Lived Inside Them

At the 4$^{th}$ month of our pregnancy I was rushed in to the hospital. I was having a miscarriage. I lost the baby about an hour later and Giovanni had informed me that it was a baby boy. I was taken to the recovery room and all I could say to Giovanni was "now we don't have to get married." He said "but I want to marry you!" The wedding went on and it was beautiful. David was a groomsman. He was right there by my side. Giovannis sisters and a close friend were my bridesmaids. Dad walked me down the ail the whole time shaking. Dad was supposed to sit down after giving me away but instead stood by my side the whole ceremony looking very proud. The only true person missing was Mom. After the ceremony we all headed to the reception in a big, white limousine I had rented for Giovanni and I.

At the reception with drinks, music and party for our loved ones and friends we entered as Mr. and Mrs. Accettola. We greeted everyone and enjoyed ourselves with dancing and great food. The Father Daughter dance meant the most to me. Mom and Dad danced at Arthur Murrays and he was a great dancer. He twirled me all over the floor and we danced until we couldn't dance anymore. David was filming and snapping pictures. There was a lot of laughter and great fun. When

# RANI

the festivities were over my now Husband and I headed to the Red Lion in Bellevue the next day.

We took our daughter Tiffany and dog PooBear and headed to Port Towson for the weekend at a very quiet lodge. As soon as we got back home Giovanni resumed his activities as if nothing had changed. While I was trying to make a good home and be the perfect wife and mother, Giovanni was going on benders week after week of drug and alcohol use. He was hanging out with his loser friends and ignoring numerous calls and pages I would make to him. I never knew where to look for him. He was all over the place.

Around 1990 Giovanni and I had the opportunity to purchase a home from one of his friends. It was going into foreclosure and we only paid what was owed to the bank. A year in a half later I got pregnant again. We were so happy. Tiffany was around 7 1/2 at this time. I was ready for a little one to be running around. I really felt this pregnancy would help Giovanni and I's marriage. It didn't. I lived a single mothers life while he ran around with other women and his friends doing drugs and living the high life.

By myself I decorated the nursery and purchased everything needed for the arrival of our new baby. During this time I opened up a business for Giovanni in Des Moines detailing cars. I felt maybe this would help our marriage if we worked together. Again I was wrong. He would never show up for work and mess up orders. It was very embarrassing. He would stay away from home sometimes up to 2 weeks.

He started seeing a girl that worked next door to the shop. She was married with 3 young boys. He would take her to all the parties and people would ask him where his wife was. Giovanni would tell everyone we were getting a divorce even though I was at home with his daughter and pregnant with our second child. I was so alone at this time. At times we wouldn't even have food in the house. We were on Food stamps and when Giovanni would get angry with me he took the Food stamps with him leaving me and Tiffany with nothing. No money, no food stamps, Nothing!

I would have to ask my Dad for help more than I would have liked. Late in my pregnancy they determined something was not right with the baby. I had several test done and it was determined that it was in distress. I was admitted into the hospital. I had to page Giovanni that it was an emergency for him to show up at the hospital. He did looking embarrassingly hung over.

The doctor started me on pertusin to induce my labor. While waiting for it to kick in Giovanni left and went to his moms house. After an hour or 2 something

# Rani

went wrong. I felt a gush of warm liquid which the doctor said was my water breaking. I felt something very warm and looked down to see a huge puddle of blood on the floor and on my sheets. I pushed the emergency button and after a nurse seen all the blood she called the doctor who had me prepped for an emergency C-section.

They asked me where my husband was and I told them he had left. The doctor seemed puzzled that I was alone and asked if I wanted him called. I said "yes." I gave them the number to his parents' house and he was called and told to rush to the hospital. All Giovanni could do was peep through a small glass window in the ER as they prepped me for sedation and C-Section. I was counting down as I looked to my left. There was a beautiful, blond young man coming towards me. He was wearing light blue scrubs. He sat next to me and took my hand. He told me "you're going to be alright, I'm going to be right here with you." "I'm not going to leave." Then I fell asleep.

The next thing I remember is waking up in a very large room the next day. I was very confused and out of it. The nurse came in to check on me and asked "how are you feeling?" I responded "tired, where's my baby?" The nurse simply said "I'll go get the doctor." Not too long afterwards the doctor came and talked to me. He asked how I was feeling and if I remembered anything. I told him I was doing better. I asked to see the Nurse that was sitting holding my hand the previous day so I could thank him for comforting me. The Doctor informed me there was no one sitting at my side during the surgery. To this day I know for a fact that God had sent me an angel to comfort me during that traumatic time. The Doctor proceeded to go on telling me he had bad and good news. I wanted the good news first. He told me the little baby boy I had was very small but doing fine. The bad news is he looks just like your husband Giovanni even down to the nose. I giggled.

I asked if I could see my baby and the Doctor told me he was in NIC-U under observation. They were going to move me into a private room soon. He said he would check on me later. I tried getting ahold of Giovanni who of course was not there with me. I couldn't so I called a close friend and told her my baby was fine though very small. I asked her if she could purchase some preemie clothes for my little guy and bring them to the hospital. The outfits I had brought to the hospital were going to be too big.

I also asked if she could try and get ahold of my husband for me and she said "of course!" The nurse came in with some food and told me to try and eat something. She put my food on the table and gave me some medication to take. She left the room and I was again all alone and I sure felt alone. Dad was on a cruise in Mexico at this time.

They moved me into a private room and I was allowed to take a small bath and change my clothes. That made me feel somewhat better. I was still in a lot of pain from the C-Section so the nurse hooked me up to a morphine pump. I was kept pretty drugged. Giovanni had flowers sent to my room though didn't show up until the next day. I was so upset but more concerned that I had not seen my baby boy that we had named Nino. The doctor came to talk to me and told me Nino had taken a toll for the worst. He had gotten Jaundice and was very sick. They wanted to transfer him to Childrens Hospital right away.

I understood though they kept me so drugged up I felt like I was in a fog. Nino was taken to Childrens Hospital and they ran all the necessary tests on him. The very next day 3 specialists came in my room to talk to me. They were all standing at the foot of my bed. It was hard to focus but I tried my best to understand what they were all there for. They started off by saying they had important news and needed my husband present. My doctor tried reaching Giovanni but was unsuccessful. All 3 doctors came back in the room and said this could not wait.

They told me my precious baby was in extreme distress and his body felt to him as though he had just ran a huge marathon. There were parts of his little organs and brain that never fully developed. They were not sure the cause and were doing the best they could to make sure Nino was getting the best care by the best doctors.

It was so hard for me to focus and listen. I could not really grasp the information they were giving me. I must have fallen asleep and I was awoken by a nurse. She asked me if I had seen my baby and I told her no. It had been 4 days. She said "your husband and daughter are down in the NIC-U visiting him." I was glad they were there. Tiffany came running into my room. I had not seen her in a few days and missed her terribly. Giovanni was out talking to the head nurse though I am not sure for what reason. They had no respect for my husband as he was not there for me this whole time.

Tiffany came running into the room and jumped on the bed. Giovanni soon followed her. He told me the baby was cute. He said he was a little yellow and small though very adorable. Soon after they left again. I am not sure why but no one from Giovannis family

# Rani

came to the hospital to visit me. My brother David and his fiancé came to see me and the baby. They had just had a baby boy 4 months prior themselves. His name was Clayton Richard. Clayton was born with a severe heart defect and was going through surgery. He had a feeding tube in his little nose. David was going through his own pain with his own little baby boy at that time. They stopped in on their way to Childrens hospital to see Nino and I.

David and his son Baby Clayton

I was so happy to have a visitor especially because it was David and Baby Clayton. They said their goodbyes then went to see Nino in the NIC-U. Nino was what we called our very precious yet very sick baby boy. The doctor came later that afternoon with a very serious look on his face. He asked if I had gone to see Nino yet and replied "no." He asked why and I said that I was scared to. The doctor informed that it was probably a good idea if I did because he was not going to make it much longer. He was put on life support that morning. He explained to me what Nino was going through and it broke my heart.

He told me he would be back later and to get some rest. Giovanni and I really needed to have a serious talk. I needed to go spend some time with Nino. I felt that if I didn't see him it wouldn't be so hard to lose him. I called Giovanni and told him our baby was not going to make it. He told me he was tinting his car windows and could not come to the hospital right now. This was so like my husband. He didn't care about anyone but himself. I felt so alone and so scared. That evening the doctor told me that Nino needed to be taken off life support and Giovanni needed to be there for them to do so. The nurse called Giovanni and was able to talk him into coming to the hospital. He arrived around 8pm. We had the dreadful talk about taking our precious boy off life support and signed the papers to approve it.

He stayed with me as they gave me medication to keep me calm and out of pain. I fell asleep for a half

# RANI

hour. The Nurse came in to take my vitals and asked if I had seen my son yet. I said no. She told me you better go see your son but I was just too scared to go. I knew if I seen him I would want to die with him. The nurse told me in a very stern voice "you're going!" "I will help you out of bed and we will walk together." Again, I said "no!" The nurse insisted I go she almost yelled "Yes, you are! We are going right now." She told me I just needed to trust her. She also told me I would thank her later. At this point there was no arguing with her.

It was a very long, cold walk to the small room Nino was in. There was a door with a glass window and in the room was my baby boy. The nurse asked me if I was alright, I said yes and we entered the room, it was nice and warm. There was a large lounge chair in the middle of the room and baby bed with a large heat lamp and lots of blankets keeping my baby warm. I could see lots of black, shiny hair as I walked up to see him for the first time in 4 days. The nurse asked if I wanted to hold him and that Nino had gotten all dressed up just to see me.

They said they had been telling him that his mommy was coming to see him. The nurse said that Nino seemed to feel less stressed when she would tell him that almost as if he knew what she was saying. She

# Secrets Behind the Four Walls
## and the Monster Mother That Lived Inside Them

handed him to me and said "he missed you." I held him for the first time in 4 days and I fell in love. I never wanted to let him go. I didn't have much time with him because they had taken him off life support and he was struggling to breathe on his own. I was so concerned that he would pass away in my arms.

The nurse asked me with a smile if I wanted her to take a picture. I said oh yes please and that ended up being a Gods blessing because I will have that forever. Giovanni showed up with our daughter Tiffany and we were all able to visit Nino for a little while more and take pictures with our precious little angel. Soon after the nurse suggested

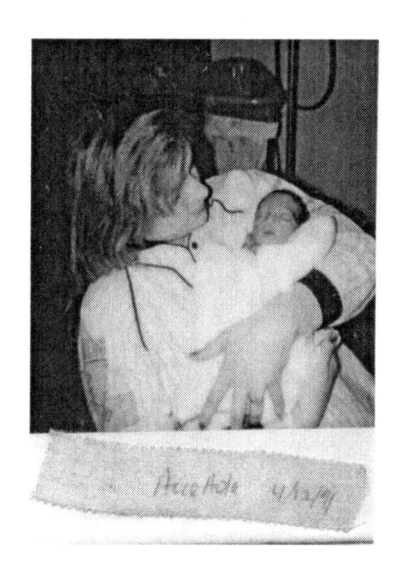

This is the picture the nurse took of me and Nino his last night alive. He went to go to be with the Lord

I go back to my room. Ninos breathing was getting more and shallower and she didn't want his fragile little soul to pass with all of us in there.

77

## RANI

I took the long, lonely, painful walk down the cold, brightly lit hallway to my room. All I wanted to do was run back, grab my baby and run out of the hospital. Once we were back in my room, I asked the nurse if Nino could spend the night with me, she said that would not be possible and that I needed to rest. Without the medicine they gave me that night, I would not of been able to sleep at all.

Early the next morning my doctor came in with the news I was dreading to hear. My precious Nino had passed away that night. Hearing those words I felt like my heart was being ripped from my body. I felt very lightheaded and thought I was going to pass out. Once again, I was all alone; Giovanni was not there for the news. I tried getting ahold of him, after calling several places I found him at his parents' house. His mom answered and all I say was "My baby died!" She calmed me down and said she would send Giovanni to the hospital right away.

***The nurse came in later that afternoon to release me from the hospital. After the doctor remove my C-section staples I was sent home, empty handed. The doctor had asked me if I would let them do an autopsy on Nino to find out all they needed about the defect he had. Still up to that point they were not sure what exactly it was that took my sons life. I said yes of course. I walked out of the Hospital doors I just entered a week earlier empty handed without my baby which was so difficult. It was a feeling that still to this day I can't really explain it, just that I felt an empty feeling in my stomach and I was empty handed.

After a few weeks they learned the disorder Nino suffered from after Giovanni and I went through a series of genetic testing. They found that we both were carriers of a very rare genetic chromosome deficiency. Around 1 in a million carry this defective gene and the fact that both of us had this identical defective gene was mind boggling. Especially being that Giovanni coming from Italy and myself born here in the States, we both met and we both have this defective gene that prevents us from having healthy babies was so crazy to me. It explained so much. I had had so many miscarriages in the process of trying to conceive and now I know why.

When I arrived home I tried very hard to put it all behind me. It took around 3 months for me to even open the beautiful nursery room I had prepared for my little angel. My aunt had to come over and tape my breasts down because they were so painful from the milk that was coming in and I had no baby to feed. It was so hard to be at home, I had Giovanni take all the baby bottles and anything that reminded me of my lost son out of the house. Eventually he also cleared out the nursery room. I though by clearing everything out of the house it would help me heal, well it didn't and I started drinking heavily to numb the pain.

Giovanni resumed his partying ways. He stayed away from home for days drinking and doing cocaine while running around as if nothing happened. I drank even more to numb the pain of my loss and the fact that I was so lonely left at home with an 8 year old, nowhere to go and no friends to visit me. I had my beautiful daughter yes but I was still so lonely with no real purpose to my life. I attended all the parents meetings, field trips, and school functions alone. I had Tiffany in ballet, tap, soccer and Campfire. I cooked new recipes I would find from library cook books trying as hard as I could to be a good mother and a good wife.

I would spend all my birthdays alone. Giovanni wouldn't even show up for Father's Day. I called one Father's Day and was told that he was at a BBQ with his friends and he hung up. He would disappoint Tiffany so many times. She missed her Father. Tiffany would try and make it better for me but she was only 8 years old and the only thing that helped was to numb myself with alcohol. So I drank and drank every day. Finally Giovanni came home and noticed how depressed I was. He told me all I needed was another baby. I got pregnant again shortly after. After telling my Doctor I was pregnant he told me he was nervous for us. He was a new Doctor and the loss of Nino was his first experience of that kind and it hit him hard.

    He told Giovanni and I we had better hope for a little girl because a girl would have a better chance of surviving the genetic defect. All through my pregnancy I was extra careful. I ate well and took very good care of myself. My doctor monitored my pregnancy very closely. During my pregnancy Giovanni started to sell cocaine as well as snort it. This made him almost permanently MIA from the home and his daughter's life. The only time I would really see him was after he had done so much cocaine he needed a place to sleep and come down from the drugs. Once he felt better he was off again with other women showing them a good time all while his pregnant wife and daughter was home alone.

    The doctor warned Giovanni that I should not be under so much stress while being pregnant and that it was not good for the baby. At that time the drugs had him so blinded that he could care less. His main concern was selling cocaine, partying with friends and having women on his arm all while driving around in his flashy low rider cars and new shoes and clothes. He was the big man on campus in the party scene. It was humiliating for me. I was so frustrated with my husband and his lifestyle that I started taking it out on Tiffany. I would yell at her, throw her in her room and be very impatient. I would hit her for no reason only to know now it was because I felt deprived of a life and the outside world felt so untouchable.

I never drank during my pregnancies so I wasn't able to numb my pain. I had to experience all the hurt I was going through and it was almost unbearable. For a short while I found myself cutting my thighs at night to feel a different pain. I had to stop because I knew my doctor would see. I tried to keep my appearance up. My hair and makeup was always done and I bought the cutest maternity clothes I could find. I wanted to stay beautiful for Giovanni but he simply wasn't interested in me.

Giovannis drinking and drugging progressively spiraled downward fast. The more he would sell the more he would do. I would find him passed out in the back office of our business sleeping hours after he was supposed to be open for business. One night Giovanni was gone I was awoken by gun shots. Four or five to be exact. Tiffany woke up scared and crying. We crawled to the kitchen to avoid getting hit. When I felt it was safe I looked out the window and realized our house just got shot up. One went through my bedroom window and two entered through the living

## Secrets Behind the Four Walls
### and the Monster Mother That Lived Inside Them

room window. I was so frightened. Again I could not get ahold of Giovanni to inform him of what had just happened. I knew it had to be drug related.

Towards the end of my pregnancy some of his friends would tell me he was cheating on me and they would ask what I was doing with him. I was so embarrassed. I didn't know what to say all I knew is I loved my husband and hoped the birth of our new baby would save our marriage and put our family back together.

On May 8, 1992 I entered the same doors of the Hospital I left a year previous empty handed with hopes of meeting my little healthy baby. They induced my labor. Giovanni was there by my side. The doctor came in to explain what they were going to do and he ordered the Pitocin to start the contractions. Around 2 hours later they broke my water and delivery was in full effect. There were 5 specialists in the room prepared for the worse. Giovanni was at my side, holding my hand but was still distracted by his ringing cellphone in his pocket. After pushing just a few times by baby Boy was born. 7lbs 5ounzes.

They let me see him only for a short moment before rushing him away to make sure he was healthy and free of the birth defect that had taken my son before. I was transported to a recovery room where my Dad was waiting for me. We announced our baby Boy

# Rani

was here and so far healthy. The doctor came in to talk to us all. He told us he looked great, a little jaundice which was normal and that the nurse would bring him in shortly to see us all.

My sweet son was so beautiful, just perfect! I was asked if I wanted to feed him for the first time. I proudly said "Yes!" He sucked the little bottle down in seconds. I swattled him and handed him to my Dad who looked so proud. Tiffany looked just as proud though also protective. I took him home the very next day. I hadn't been this happy since I brought my baby girl home 9 years earlier. Giovanni gathered all the flowers and cards and with our baby boy in my arms we all went home together. We decided to name our son, Giovanni Richard Junior. On our way out the Doctor came up to us to congratulate us and tell us how

Giovanni Jr. my son, my blessing.

happy he was that we were able take our baby home this time.

Giovanni looked at me as we walked out and said "see, you aren't leaving empty handed this time." At that moment I felt nothing but pure happiness and hope there was just a half a chance for change and that we would be a happy family now. Well it didn't. When we arrived home, Giovanni helped me into the house and said he was leaving to get some snacks for us. He didn't return for 3 days. I had my baby and he was healthy and that was all that mattered to me at that time. I wanted a perfect home for Tiffany and Giovanni JR. I was sure that having a new baby boy would change some of Giovannis ways but it didn't.

The drinking and drugging continued with a vengeance. He kept all the money from us locked in a safe and only gave me barely enough to get by. My drinking slowly returned leaving Tiffany to take care of Giovanni JR most the time. I pulled away from Tiffany because I was ashamed. I was always so astonished at how Giovanni could party daily and forget about the beautiful little family he neglected at home. On rare occasions he would show up, usually on Sundays which I called "family days" to the children. I noticed Tiffany started looking forward to the "family days" because she missed her dad and knew she would see

# Rani

us together on those days. Going to the Seattle Center, Green Lake or the ocean, making a full day of normalcy as if everything was ok just for one day this seemed to be routine.

My drinking increased as well. I would drink myself into a black out and leave the house. One night I drove and parked in a 711 with no recollection of how I got there. Giovannis brother found me and took me home. The next day my Dad came over and arranged for me to go to treatment for 21 days. Giovanni was left to take care of an 11year old and 2 year old all while fighting his own addictions himself. It was hard for me because I would call home and Tiffany would answer. She was left home alone with Giovanni JR most of the time.

Dad, Giovanni and the kids came every weekend to visit. The kids looked a mess and Tiffany always looked tired. I could tell things at home were not good. This unsettled me so much. I told Dad I did not want to return to that house and that I wanted to make other arrangements for the kids and I. Dad said he would help me with that. When Giovanni found out he came to the treatment center and convinced me things would change and get better. He promised not to drink or do drugs, I believed him.

The day I returned home, he left with a friend and

## Secrets Behind the Four Walls
### and the Monster Mother That Lived Inside Them

it all started all over again. It was a lifestyle to him and something he was unable to change due to his own demons. I started to like the fact he wasn't there. I wouldn't call him at all. I liked making my house my home. I cooked fancy meals for the kids and would take them on bike rides around the neighborhood. We dressed up for Halloweens and would go to Dads to Trick-or-Treat. This went on for a few years. I never attended the AA meetings that were suggested to me so slowly alcohol found its way back into my life. Giovanni was getting tired of the drinking and drug scene and wanted to make a change. We thought it would be good to start fresh in a new environment so in 1997 we sold our house.

I found a beautiful home in a nice neighborhood close to Dads house in Federal Way. We moved in, purchased all new furniture and made this house our home. It was perfect. Giovanni JR quickly made friends with all the little boys close to his age. They were always at the house jumping on the trampoline or playing ninjas like little boys do. Tiffany became best friends with the girl next door whose name was also Tiffany and her exact age. We had perfect neighbors. One side there was an attractive couple our age with kids our kids' age. Giovanni and I started hanging out with them on the weekends having cocktails and bomb fires in the backyard.

Giovanni was still gone at times but it wasn't as bad. I didn't feel alone like I did at the old house. I had my close friend next door who would come over and keep me company. Shortly, the neighbors started to notice Giovanni being gone for days on end. They would ask me where my husband was all the time and all I could do was shrug it off. I was embarrassed and didn't know what to say. They seemed to have perfect, normal, non-addicted husbands home with them every night. This became more painful for me so I slowly isolated myself like I did at the old house. I thought by doing this people could not see my marriage was so unstable.

Finally he lost his business in Des Moines from all the drinking and drugs. I got a settlement from a fast food restaurant and we talked about opening a new business together in Burien. This time we work together. We went to work together and home together and for a while this worked great. Around this time Giovanni lost his favorite uncle. Something happened to him shortly after the funeral. He started staying home and cut way back on the heavy drinking and drug use. We even went on walks together. For a short time I felt we had a perfect marriage. He was there on

## Secrets Behind the Four Walls
### and the Monster Mother That Lived Inside Them

Tiffany's Prom night looking at is beautiful, maturing baby girl proudly. He went to all Giovanni's JRs baseball game and Judo competitions.

In my eyes things were great; we were only hanging out with our married couple friends and having family time with the kids. What I wasn't aware of is that Giovanni was still associating with the married girl he had met years before while working in Des Moines. One night I had listened to his voice messages and heard her telling him to come over because her husband was at work. When I confronted him about it he simply told me she was a nuisance and I fell for it. I wanted to keep things the way they were so I didn't make a big deal and brushed it under the rug.

Around 2001 I opened an Espresso Stand in Des Moines. It had been my dream for a long time and finally it came true. I worked very hard and trained Tiffany to work for me while she was attending College. She had moved out of the house shortly after turning 19 and needed extra money. I was running the stand while Giovanni ran the Custom Auto business in Burien. We no longer went to work together so he slowly started associating with the wrong people again. We still managed to make it work for around a year and then we both started hanging out with my younger brother Sam who partied like a rock star doing cocaine and drinking every weekend.

I started doing cocaine myself and immediately loved it. Cocaine made drinking less desirable. I could drink and drink without getting drunk. I got a lot done around the house and it just became the thing to do every weekend, turning into every day.

One occasion while lying in bed Giovanni's phone rang. He quickly answered then got all ready and left saying he would be right back and bring us some food. He was gone for close to 3 weeks. I didn't hear from him once. No phone call or anything. He didn't even open the shop for those 3 weeks he had one of his drug friends running it. I had no clue of any of this. I knew he wasn't dead and that he was most likely binging because of his past behavior. I must say, those 3 weeks were actually good for me. I drank some but was not using Cocaine at all. I actually felt health and loved working at my espresso stand. It was cheerful all the time.

In this process I developed a crush on my married neighbor. I was like a little school girl. He would drive by the stand every morning and evening to and from work and every now and them stop in for a coffee and chat. I would watch him in his yard doing yard work and working around his house. We both really liked

## Secrets Behind the Four Walls
### and the Monster Mother That Lived Inside Them

each other but never took the crush any further. This made the fact that my husband was gone easier for me.

My business started to struggle because I was trying to balance being a single parent and a business owner all in one. I had to close the stand to take Giovanni JR to and from school which made me lose a ton of business. I tried hiring some help so I never had to close. I prepared for the town parade for around a week. I knew this would be one of our busiest days and I was very excited. I put tables with bright umbrellas out on my porch and the line was out the door that hot, summer, cheerful day in July. Giovanni called my cellphone that morning after 3 weeks. He asked if Giovanni JR was with me and if he could come watch the parade at my stand. He spoke with Giovanni Junior for a while then JR handed the phone back to me.

He told me he missed me and I missed him too. He showed up later that afternoon while I was visiting with an old best friend of mine and her daughter. The stand had been extremely busy and Tiffany was working hard for me. Giovanni stayed in his car tell I walked over to talk to him. He got out and gave me a long hug, told me I looked beautiful which I did. I felt the best I had felt in a very long time. It felt nice to be sober, healthy and running a successful business. I thought I could go on with my life without

# RANI

my husband but standing there looking at him I was glad to see him and I didn't care about the previous 3 weeks at that very moment.

He asked if he could come back home and of course I said "yes but things had to change." Giovanni was worried some about our neighbor friends and what they would think. I explained that I didn't care what anyone thought; I just wanted my family back together and healthy. We were supposed to meet each other back at home after the parade. I got there first so I cleaned up and lit some candles so the house would look nice. I made a cocktail and waited for my husband. It was nice and calm in the house. Giovanni JR had a friend over and they were watching a movie. I hadn't had my husband home in 3 weeks so being alone was starting to be my normal.

He finally arrived after dark, with a chip on his shoulder. He was no longer sorry as he was earlier that day. I wanted to talk about where he had been for the last almost month and why he didn't call. We fought a while about it and I finally left. After returning he was again sorry. I told him I didn't want to talk about anything negative. We needed to move on and move forward if we were going to work on our marriage. It never crossed my mind that he was with another woman; I

## SECRETS BEHIND THE FOUR WALLS
### and the Monster Mother That Lived Inside Them

just thought he was binging with some loser friends as he had done so many times before in our relationship.

Things with us got better but only because we had a common addiction. I wanted to keep my husband at home so I started to be his drinking and drugging buddy. I knew if I drank and did cocaine with him he would stay home with me. By this point we had to close both our businesses and were struggling for money. Giovanni would do odd jobs and sell things to support us and our drug habit. He would give me cocaine and then leave to his friend's house.

Around this time my grandpa got sick and entered the hospital down in Centralia. It was decided by the family that I should take Grandpa home to live with me. I did. I became the power of attorney to his estate and responsible for all his bills and care. I was responsible for getting his house ready to sell. It was extremely hard because he had lived there since the 1970s and never updates anything or got rid of anything. There was a lot of stuff in the house I had to sell so I held many garage sales while Grandpa was recovering.

Time came to take Grandpa home so we set him up downstairs in our house. He was very demanding and needed 24hour supervision. I couldn't leave the house; I was trapped 24-7. I drank quite a bit during this time. I knew I could not meet his needs as they should be met so I found him a beautiful, new senior home with 24hour care. I was finally free but not before falling into a very deep depression. Giovanni and I started spending more and more time together which meant more and more drinking and cocaine use.

So with the money my grandfather gave me I spent on cocaine and the high life. We would do cocaine and if I wasn't doing cocaine I was sleeping all day. I would stay up for days cleaning my house. My love affair for Cocaine took over my life quickly. I felt invincible. I had money to play with, my house was spot less, and I had friends over all the time. I lost touch with my children. Mostly Tiffany. I barely saw her and didn't even realize it. I missed family functions and I even missed a birthday dinner my daughter prepared for me at her apartment.

All with no remorse. All that mattered was my next fix. Cocaine made me feel as though I had no care in the world all while my life was crumbling around me. This went on for a good 2 years. At my worse I suffered some kind mental break down. Personally I feel a demon got a hold of me and wouldn't let go. My breakdown manifested itself on a summer camping trip, the last one I would take with Dad before he passed away from Cancer.

I no longer could function normally. I couldn't

# SECRETS BEHIND THE FOUR WALLS
## and the Monster Mother That Lived Inside Them

touch anything I felt was dirty such as clothes, dishes or anything with dust on it. The hardest part was I was afraid to shower, to wear my clothes more than once, or use my makeup more than once. My home became something out of a horror movie and so was my life. I threw away just about everything I thought had bugs on them. Almost every other night I would spray my house down with bleach. I went through a small fortune buying antibacterial sprays, Lysol, Pinesol and bleach. Everything I could to kill the bugs I thought I seen living all over my house and body. The situation became unbearable.

My family told me they could no longer live this way. All the while I was drinking and doing cocaine to have the energy to clean, clean, clean. During this dark time in my life my son was attending West Valley church and was very involved in church events, youth group and Young Life. That was his escape from the hell he was living in. I would be up from cocaine and cleaning as my sweet son would be leaving for church. He spent a lot of time with his youth leaders and eventually became one himself. Giovanni JR set up his own baptism at his church and told Giovanni and I it would mean a lot to him if we attended the service.

We sat proudly in the first row. I never was so happy, he looked so wonderful. The people of the church came up to Giovanni and I and told us just how special Giovanni JR was and what a great person he was. I fell in love with that church that day. I didn't go back though; I was still in the throes of my addiction and mental breakdown.

Around August of 2007 we found out Dad had 12 days to live. I would visit Dad in the hospital only to be treated horribly my Lynn the whole time. She made sure to make me feel uncomfortable and unwelcome. She was so rude to Tiffany and Giovanni one day that they left Dads hospital room crying and that really upset him since they were the 2 people Dad loved the most in this world. They sent Dad home to pass away. Lynn made it almost impossible to visit him but Dad would call when he could and rush me over to see him. She would be furious to see me there so she started hiding the phone so Dad couldn't call me.

When Dad passed away it threw me further into drugs and alcohol. Giovanni and I hung out every weekend with my half-brother Sam doing cocaine and more cocaine. One night of extreme drug use I called out to God. "Please help me!" I grabbed a bible and just started to cry out to God. Something came over me and I knew at that moment God had heard my cry. I started to pray with every TV minister I could find. I kept the channel on TBN Christian channel and that

# SECRETS BEHIND THE FOUR WALLS
## and the Monster Mother That Lived Inside Them

was all I watched. I was so hungry for the word of the Lord and the new life I felt God would give me.

I told my husband I wanted to change my life with or without him. He also wanted to quit all the drugs and drinking. Very quickly God answered our prayers and we set out for a new way of living. It wasn't overnight all though it felt like it was. Giovanni and I started attending West Valley Church with our son, going to morning breakfast, bible study and Sunday service. The drugs would pop up a few more times though it was just God testing us. Eventually the addiction left our bodies. We threw ourselves in the Church, never missing a Sunday. Giovanni JR and Tiffany were finally proud of us and we were proud of ourselves.

Around the time I was changing my life Lynn never told me where Dad was buried nor had a funeral for him. This is still very painful for me. She tried so very hard to keep him away from me in life and did the same in his death. My sobriety has been tested on more than one occasion but my love for the Lord helps me know I am stronger then my addiction. I will never forget when God took my hand and gave me mercy when I thought I didn't deserve it. God continues to walk me out of the line of fire each time. He has taken hold of my family and has not let go. I can say I

# Rani

feel strong and healthy and no longer ashamed. I have been washed clean in the blood of Jesus.

Giovanni and I set out to find jobs. We went over to Tiffanys apartment and she helped her Dad fill out an online job application for Sams Club. No more than 1 week later he was called in for an interview. Giovanni got his first real job in 40 years sober and clean. He was scared though determined. We knew this was another gift from God. After 3 weeks of working he asked his manager if there was a position available for his wife. I went in met with her and a month later I was working in the bakery. Another gift from God. A year later I received a small gift from Dads will and was able to fix my home with new furniture, paint and life! I was finally able to erase the signs of my illness that had pledged me and my husband for so long.

Giovanni and I are strong Christians and members of West Valley Church. Giovanni got hired as a long shore-man and is still also working at Sams Club part time. I am lead baker and very proud. Giovanni and I have never again missed a family event and even throw them at our house sober. No longer am I ashamed of myself, my house, my husband! Giovanni and I have a normal, healthy marriage. We are never apart and love each other deeply. Finally we have the respect of our children, family, friends and co-workers. Most of all we have the love of Jesus Christ.

April of 2011 Tiffany blessed our family with a new addition. A sweet, precious baby girl Corynn Rain. I believe she was Gods gift to our family for our change, love and devotion to him as our Savior. Giovanni Junior is a lead drummer in his Christain Rock band reaching out to teens and young adults through music. He is a regular member of West Valley Church and is a Youth Leader.

Writing this book has been hard yet healing and a long time coming. I wrote this as my testimony to the grace of God and the love he has for all of us. No matter who you are or what situation you find yourself in, all you have to do is give it all to God and he will take you in the direction you never thought in a million years to go.

Surrender, cry out, ask God to please rescue you and allow him in your heart. Jesus Christ is the Messiah, the King of Kings. God is my Savior and I live to serve him! Thank you for letting me share my story

GOD BLESS!

My Dad

We are strong in faith and
in love.

THE END!